Paint a watercolour landscape in minutes

ATMOSPHERE, MOOD and LIGHT

Keith Fenwick

ATMOSPHERE, MOOD and LIGHT

Dedication:

*To Dorothy, my wife, for her support, advice and typing of
the text, and to all my students over the years whose needs
have helped me to determine the content of this book.*

This edition published 2002

Copyright © Arcturus Publishing Limited
1–7 Shand Street, London SE1 2ES

Distributed to the trade and art markets in North
America by North Light Books
an imprint of F & W Publications, Inc.
4700 East Galbraith Road
Cincinnati, OH 45236
(800) 289-0963

ISBN 1-58180-392-3

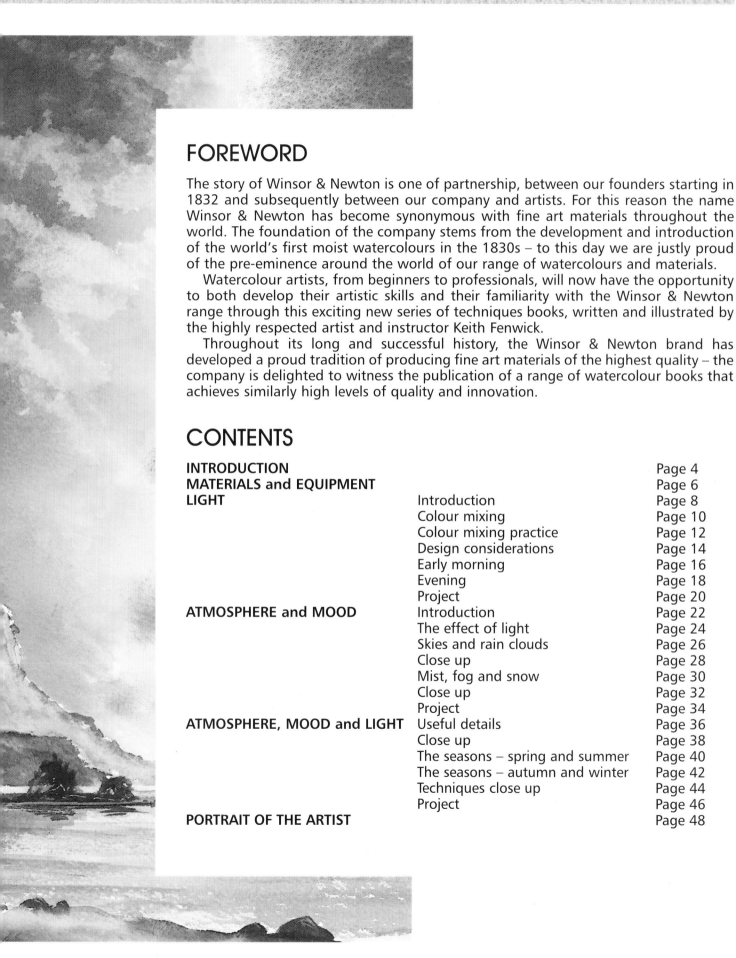

FOREWORD

The story of Winsor & Newton is one of partnership, between our founders starting in 1832 and subsequently between our company and artists. For this reason the name Winsor & Newton has become synonymous with fine art materials throughout the world. The foundation of the company stems from the development and introduction of the world's first moist watercolours in the 1830s – to this day we are justly proud of the pre-eminence around the world of our range of watercolours and materials.

Watercolour artists, from beginners to professionals, will now have the opportunity to both develop their artistic skills and their familiarity with the Winsor & Newton range through this exciting new series of techniques books, written and illustrated by the highly respected artist and instructor Keith Fenwick.

Throughout its long and successful history, the Winsor & Newton brand has developed a proud tradition of producing fine art materials of the highest quality – the company is delighted to witness the publication of a range of watercolour books that achieves similarly high levels of quality and innovation.

CONTENTS

ATMOSPHERE, MOOD and LIGHT

INTRODUCTION

Light is the single most important factor in all painting. It's the effect of light and shade that gives reality and expression to paintings; it also helps to establish structure, illuminate colour and highlight textures. The addition of shadows and the variety of tones add interest and prevent a painting looking flat.

For your paintings to work visually, you will need to draw and paint the features, capture the direction of light, vary your tonal values to emphasize the light and, of course, emulate the light itself. Light makes the landscape real and believable. Without it, the landscape wouldn't exist as we know it.

Glazing techniques are useful for creating the effects of light, but too many glazes can destroy transparency. Experience will demonstrate that the greatest source of light is the white of the paper. Atmosphere and mood add extra quality to paintings, making them special.

Skies are an important aspect in creating atmosphere and mood – after all, they can represent almost two-thirds of a painting. Skies painted using diagonal brush strokes suggest a sense of movement. Soft, fluffy cumulus clouds suggest the peace and tranquillity of a summer's day. Dark nimbus clouds are synonymous with a feeling of awe. A colourful evening sky can create a feeling of contentment.

As artists we don't necessarily paint what we see. We attempt to capture a moment in time that stirs within us, a particular feeling about a subject or landscape. In the following pages I will show you techniques and approaches you can use to translate that feeling into a finished watercolour.

Keith H Fenwick

The sky in **Boatyard** fascinated me. The rays of light were created by removing paint from the surface of the paper by rubbing gently with an eraser, taking care not to damage the surface of the paper.

ATMOSPHERE, MOOD and LIGHT *Materials and equipment*

INTRODUCTION
A visit to the local art store can be a confusing experience. My preference is to use quality materials, and I would advise you to do the same. Purchase the best you can afford. It will work out cheaper in the long run and save you a great deal of frustration.

PAINTS
Most professional artists prefer tube colours because they are moist and more convenient for mixing large washes of colour. Pans of paint become very hard if left unused and release less colour.

The choice of colours is personal to the artist, but you won't go far wrong if you begin with my basic range. This comprises:

SKIES	Payne's Gray Cerulean Blue French Ultramarine Indanthrene Blue Alizarin Crimson Winsor Red Cobalt Blue	LIGHT	Gold Ochre Winsor Yellow Cadmium Yellow Pale Raw Sienna The white of the paper
EARTH	Raw Sienna Burnt Sienna Cadmium Yellow Pale Permanent Sap Green Gold Ochre Winsor Yellow Burnt Umber	ATMOSPHERE and MOOD	Payne's Gray Alizarin Crimson Cerulean Blue French Ultramarine Raw Sienna Burnt Umber
		MIXERS	Cadmium Yellow Pale Permanent Sap Green Gold Ochre

PALETTE
All artists have their own way of painting. I prefer to use a large open palette. I simply draw my colours into the centre of the palette and mix them to my requirements. For large washes I premix colours in saucers. The palette shown includes a lid which provides more than ample space for mixing colours.

BRUSHES
For painting skies and other large areas, I use a 1½in hake brush and for control a size 14 round. For buildings and angular elements, such as mountains and rocks, I use a ¾in flat. For fine detail, such as tree structures, I use a size 3 rigger (originally developed for painting ships' rigging, hence the name) and for detailed work, shadows etc, I use a size 6 round.

PAPERS

Quality papers come in different forms, sizes, textures and weights. Paper can also be purchased in gummed pads, spiral bound pads, blocks (glued all around except for an area where the sheets can be separated) and in varying sizes and textures.

I prefer to purchase my paper in sheet form (30in x 22in) and cut it to the appropriate size. The paintings in this book were painted on 200 or 300lb rough textured watercolour paper. When sketching outdoors, I use spiral bound pads.

Winsor & Newton offer a choice of surfaces and weights, as follows:

HP (Hot pressed) has a smooth surface, used for calligraphy and pen and wash.

NOT (Cold pressed) has a slight texture (called 'the tooth') and is used for traditional watercolour paintings.

ROUGH paper has a more pronounced texture which is wonderful for large washes, tree foliage, sparkle on water, dry brush techniques, etc. I always use a rough textured paper.

Paper can be purchased in different imperial weights (the weight of a ream (500 sheets), size 30in x 22in):

90lb/190gsm is thin and light; unless wetted and stretched, it cockles very easily when washes are applied.

140lb/300gsm paper doesn't need stretching unless very heavy washes are applied.

200lb/425gsm or 300lb/640gsm papers are my preference.

OTHER ITEMS

The following items make up my painting kit:

Tissues: For creating skies, applying textures and cleaning palettes.

Mediums: Art Masking Fluid, Permanent Masking Medium, Granulation Medium and Lifting Preparation are all useful and selectively used in my paintings.

Masking tape: To control the flow of paint, masking areas in the painting and for fastening paper to backing board. I prefer ¾in width as it is easier to remove.

Cocktail sticks: Useful for applying masking when fine lines are required.

Grease-proof paper: For applying masking.

Atomizer bottle: For spraying paper with clean water or paint.

Painting board: Your board should be 2 inches larger all round than the size of your watercolour painting. Always secure your paper at each corner and each side (8 places) to prevent it cockling when you are painting.

Eraser: A putty eraser is ideal for removing masking.

Sponge: Natural sponges are useful for removing colour and creating tree foliage, texture on rocks, etc.

Water-soluble crayons: For drawing outlines, correcting mistakes and adding highlights.

Palette knife: For moving paint around on the paper (see page 32).

Saucers: For mixing large washes and pouring paint.

Hairdryer: For drying paint between stages.

Easel and stool: I occasionally use a lightweight easel and a stool for outdoor work.

LIGHT *Introduction*

Artists of all generations have endeavoured to capture the magical effects of light on the landscape. Watercolour painting is ideal for this by providing contrasting tonal values and colour, wet into wet and the ability to incorporate both hard and soft edges.

Coloured glazes consisting of a small amount of paint and lots of water can easily be applied, either to warm up sections of a painting to represent sunlight or to provide contrast by applying cool colours.

It's important to realize that the white of the paper and the transparency of watercolour provide the greatest source of light in a watercolour painting. A source of light can be brightened by surrounding it with darker contrasting tones of colour. You can prove this for yourself: take a piece of waste watercolour paper, paint your light source, then paint dark tones of colour around it. If you do this your light source will appear lighter.

To begin with it's a good idea to select your subject and produce simple tonal studies to visualize the effects of light on your landscape. If you paint your subject at different times of the day, you will experience the effect changing light has on the landscape. The knowledge you get from these exercises will be invaluable for your paintings.

The colours I find most useful are shown below.

Payne's Gray

Cadmium Yellow Pale

Cerulean Blue

Alizarin Crimson

Raw Sienna

Burnt Umber

In **Evening Light** I used various tonal values in the clouds on the right and left lighter areas surrounding the large tree, to emphasize its structure. I painted cloud shadows in the foreground to provide contrast with the soft light in the sky.

Moonlight provides a good example of light in the landscape. The soft light radiates over the distant mountains and highlights the farmstead and the track, leading the viewer's eye into the painting. Masking fluid was initially applied to preserve the white of the paper representing the track. Washes and detail were applied after the masking fluid was removed.

Practice

- Study the examples in this book and practise painting wet into wet skies to represent the various light situations.
- Practise colour mixing, using the colours specified in the text.
- Practise using an eraser to remove colour, creating shafts of light as in a woodland glade or an atmospheric sky.

LIGHT *Colour mixing*

Colour has fascinated artists for generations. Many books have been written about this subject but there's no substitute for experience. I'm often asked by my students to divulge the percentages of each hue I have mixed together to achieve a particular colour, but I can't tell them. I just mix quantities of each colour together until I am satisfied with the outcome. Certain rules obviously have to be followed. If fresh clean colours are required, it's best to mix only two colours together. For more subtle shades, mix three colours together. If you mix more than three colours you are likely to end up with a dull colour. Artists call this 'mud', but there may be occasions when this is precisely what is needed.

THE BASICS OF COLOUR MIXING

The primary colours are red, yellow and blue. If similar quantities of each primary colour are mixed together the result is almost a black colour, as shown in the colour circle left. If blue and yellow are mixed together, they will produce green. Mixing red and yellow gives orange, while mixing red and blue results in a violet or purple colour. These mixtures are known as secondary colours. Tertiary colours are created by mixing a primary colour with a secondary colour; any red, yellow and blue will suffice. It's easy, as the next exercise shows.

Follow the arrows in the colour circle. By using three primary colours in the above combinations with various amounts of water, a wide range of tints can be produced. Of course, a vast range of colours can be bought, but there's nothing like experimenting with the basics to discover the range of tones you can produce.

Some colour combinations I find useful are shown below.

Cerulean Blue and Alizarin Crimson –
Shadows over snow

Raw Sienna and Alizarin Crimson –
Under-painting for evening sky

Payne's Gray and Alizarin Crimson –
Cloud colours for evening sky

Payne's Gray and Cerulean Blue –
Rain clouds

Payne's Gray and Raw Sienna –
Mist and fog

My basic palette of colours is shown below. The beginner won't go far wrong if they begin with this selection. Additional colours I use to support my basic palette are also shown below. I call these extra colours my 'supportive' palette. Occasionally, I may select further colours from the wide range available.

Basic palette: Payne's Gray, Cerulean Blue, Alizarin Crimson, Raw Sienna, Burnt Sienna, Burnt Umber, Cadmium Yellow Pale, Permanent Sap Green.

Supportive palette: French Ultramarine, Indanthrene Blue, Quinacridone Red, Winsor Yellow, Brown Madder Alizarin, Gold Ochre.

Payne's Gray and Alizarin Crimson – storm clouds

Alizarin Crimson and Cerulean Blue – cloud colours

Payne's Gray and Burnt Umber – storm clouds

French Ultramarine and Cadmium Yellow Pale – light in the sky

Storm clouds – Payne's Gray and Alizarin Crimson, painted over a pale Raw Sienna wash.

Light on the landscape – French Ultramarine on the right and French Ultramarine/Alizarin Crimson on the left, painted over a Cadmium Yellow Pale under-painting.

11

LIGHT Colour Mixing *Practice*

I've included this woodland scene, **Coat of Many Colours**, to provide you with an opportunity to practise your colour mixing. I would like you to note the variations in tone throughout this painting – this variation is important. The tree grouping on the left side of the painting has been painted in darker tones, leading the eye beyond it and into the distance.

AUTUMN TREES

In this grouping you will observe a wide range of green and autumn tints. The greens have been created by using Cerulean Blue mixed with Cadmium Yellow Pale and Raw Sienna. The autumn hues have been mixed using combinations of Raw Sienna, Burnt Sienna and Alizarin Crimson.

Trees and bushes appear dark on the inside and become lighter towards the extremities. To capture this depth in the foliage, I over-painted with dark tones of Payne's Gray mixed with a little Alizarin Crimson when the under-painting was completely dry, producing a dark mauve colour. Never use black for this purpose – it really kills a painting.

The tree structures were painted using a weak Burnt Umber, followed by stippling in the foliage with a small, artist's sponge, incorporating suitable autumn colours. Before you try this, practise first on a similarly textured piece of watercolour paper.

ADDING DARKER TONES

To create the foliage on the left-hand trees, I applied a wide range of greens in varying tones, mixed from Cerulean Blue, Cadmium Yellow and Raw Sienna. To paint the foliage, I stippled with the sponge dipped in paint, pre-mixed on my palette. When this was completely dry, I over-stippled with dark tones of a Payne's Gray/Alizarin Crimson mix to create depth in the foliage. Depth is so necessary to the success of a painting such as this, because it leads the eye beyond the darker tree grouping into the distance. This concept or design principle is known as 'recession'.

When the paint was dry I added some white gouache paint to the green mixtures to lighten them. Using the stippling technique, I added a few highlights in the foliage to retain the overall impression of depth.

TEXTURE

Your painting can be made more realistic by adding texture to the grassy areas. This is achieved by applying initial washes of a soft pale yellow in the distance, followed by green to selected areas. When the paint is approximately half dry, the edge of a hake (the tip of the brush should be brought almost to a chisel edge) is used to paint in some darker tones to represent texture; loading the brush with a Payne's Gray/Alizarin Crimson mix is ideal for this. You must touch the paper lightly to deposit paint, then, using the corner of the brush, flick upwards to create tufts of grass. It's a very simple technique.

The walkers are important in this painting – they're the focal point, leading your eye down the path. Don't forget to paint some shadows across the footpath.

LIGHT *Design considerations*

When I first began painting, I often completed paintings that looked boring although drawn correctly and well designed. After studying works of art in national galleries, I soon realized that my paintings needed light to give them life. Light is the single most important factor in all paintings.

When I'm unhappy with a painting, I will shine a powerful torch over it to determine whether making areas lighter will improve my representation. Then I wash out the colour with a sponge and dab it with a tissue until I feel I've created the effect I'm looking for. Try this technique – it works.

Although I still use this technique, I attempt to plan for it before I apply paint. Paintings don't just happen, they have to be designed. Keep the following points in mind when you are planning your painting.

Points to Remember

1. *In early morning light, shadows are ill-defined, the elements lack sharpness and colours have a bluish appearance.*

2. *When the sun is setting every feature in the landscape – eg, buildings, trees, etc – will appear as silhouettes against the sky.*

3. *Glazes can be applied to warm certain areas of a painting to represent sunlight.*

Winter's Majesty is a very simple exercise for you to try. Note the cold winter sky, the splashes of colour in the foliage and the sense of recession, achieved by painting the far distant trees in pale cool colours wet into wet. Observe the subtle sky shadows in the snow and the impression of stubble here and there. The figures are the focal point. The tree structures were scratched out with a palette knife and cocktail stick when the paint was one-third dry.

There's something special about light attempting to show through the diffused background of early morning mist. The atmospheric effect makes it difficult to see the real colours of objects in the distance.

In the middle distance, colours appear bluer, less sharply defined and lighter in tone, no matter how much light there is. As we approach the foreground the elements appear sharper and darker in tone than they do in the distance. Although their true colours are displayed, foreground objects can appear simply as silhouettes if the distant light is bright.

In **The Hikers** *the principles of design we addressed above are clearly represented. The light is attempting to break through the mist and the distant mountains are diffused and cool in colour. The path leads the eye into the painting and the hikers become the focal point. More detail has been painted in the foreground, with the rocks created by outlining their shape with brushwork and their structure scratched out with a palette knife.*

Autumn on the Lake *was a simple sketch produced in six minutes. The group of trees is virtually a silhouette, but colour reflects across the loch as the sun rises above the distant mountains. This is a useful exercise for a beginner.*

LIGHT *Early morning*

Here are three different examples of early morning light: first light as dawn breaks; a back-lit subject where the light has broken through the clouds, creating a glow over distant mountains; and a front-lit woodland scene.

Skylight *is a fine example of early morning sun breaking through the clouds, lighting up the landscape. The distant mountain seems to sparkle, as does the surface of the water. The sky is the main feature in this painting, although it was painted in less than three minutes. Initially, I painted a circle of Cadmium Yellow Pale. While the paper was flat, I painted French Ultramarine on the right-hand side and a Payne's Gray/Alizarin Crimson mix on the left.*

Using a spray bottle, I sprayed water in the centre of the Cadmium Yellow Pale and, lifting up the board, tilted the paper to allow the colours to run in different directions and blend together. An occasional spray here and there encouraged the paint to flow freely. When I was satisfied with the cloud formation, I laid the board perfectly flat to allow the paint to dry. When approximately one-third dry, I used an absorbent tissue to add a few white clouds.

Boathouse *was painted at the first light of dawn. The background is a simple wash of varying light tones of Payne's Gray over a weak Raw Sienna under-painting. The distant trees were painted wet into wet to achieve a soft diffused look. The foreground trees are in silhouette. The red roof of the boathouse is quite dull, as is the pale coloured stonework. The lake surface reflects the colours of the sky and the water on the left-hand side is in shadow from the dark tree grouping. The boat was added to give a splash of colour to this otherwise dull scene.*

River Rhapsody is the type of scene I love to paint. The subdued early morning light was behind me, attempting to break through the early morning mist. The far distant trees can barely be seen and blurred images of the trees in the middle distance provide a background to the large trees on the left.

It's autumn, the leaves have fallen, allowing the structure of the trees to be visible. Distant tree structures were scratched out with the palette knife. If the paint is too wet when scratched out it will run back, resulting in a dark tree structure. The trick is to leave the paint until it is about one-third dry, when a pleasing light tree structure will result. In this painting some structures are light and others dark.

The trunks of the large trees in the foreground were painted in dark tones of brown and a tissue shaped to a point wiped down to remove paint, lightening the right-hand side of the trunks. A rigger brush was used to paint some dark tones on the trunks, making them look round. The branches were added – also using a rigger brush – and a few reflections painted in the water.

Very important in this painting are the contrasts of pale tones and colours representing the soft, diffused early morning atmosphere.

LIGHT *Evening*

Evening is probably my favourite time to paint. The landscape is going to sleep. It's so peaceful, a time for contemplation. The clouds have darkened, contrasting with the light in the sky, making the light appear even brighter. The sky colours are reflected on the surface of the water, creating a sense of peace and tranquillity.

In **Lone Sailor** *the silhouettes of the foreground rocks and the sailor contrast with the fading light.*

I want you to use your imagination to try to capture this scene in paint. Don't try to copy the colours I have used exactly. Use them only as guides. Make the painting your own. Have some fun with it.

Soft Light contrasts with the painting above, the light soft and diffused, providing a glowing background to this autumn scene. I painted the sky by initially applying a pale Raw Sienna wash to wet the whole of the painting. In the sky, I brushed in soft purple mixes made from Payne's Gray and Alizarin Crimson, adding lots of water to produce the pastel colours. While the paint was still wet, I brushed in some pale grey to represent distant trees.

The ivy covering the base of the trees was painted by stippling various green tones with a round headed hog-hair brush. This brush was also used to stipple in the foreground texture after the initial wash had dried. (For detailed instructions on painting tree structures, see page 43.)

The sea is calm, the day's fishing is over and the light is quickly fading. The scene depicted in **Resting** was completed in 40 minutes on the coastal road near Mallaig in Scotland.

An initial Raw Sienna wash was applied to the sky area with a hake brush. I added a little Alizarin Crimson as I worked towards the horizon. When the under-painting was approximately one-third dry, the clouds were painted using mixes of Payne's Gray and Alizarin Crimson. The same colours were used to paint the water.

The boat was added to balance the darker cloud formations in the left-hand side of the painting, but it's the sky that establishes the atmosphere and mood.

The treetops and a distant field are illuminated in **Moonlight**. I began by painting the full moon with masking fluid. When this was completely dry, I painted the sky by wetting the paper with clean water, using the hake brush, and followed this with washes of French Ultramarine with a little Alizarin Crimson added. A tissue was used to create a few white cloud shapes. When the rest of the painting was completed, the masking was removed and the shadows on the moon were painted. Note that the path was painted by retaining the white of the paper and adding a little colour here and there. It's an important feature, leading the eye into the painting and up to the moon.

Walk on the Beach shows a glorious sky lighting up the landscape. I used a range of colours to capture it. In addition to soft Cerulean Blue and Raw Sienna, with a touch of Gold Ochre for the under-painting, I used a combination of Payne's Gray/Cerulean Blue and Burnt Sienna for the clouds. A tissue was used to soften the edges and create a few white clouds. The sea was painted with a hake brush. I painted the rocks initially by applying washes and then created the shapes by moving paint with a palette knife. Note the shadows over the sand – such little touches improve a painting.

LIGHT *Project*

The scene depicted in **The Garden in Bloom** is one that I felt I just had to paint, as a reminder of my visit to Bodnant Gardens in Wales. The soft blue sky contrasted beautifully with the colourful azaleas and rhododendrons. I remember sitting on a seat, thinking how peaceful it was. The painting provided the opportunity to use some imaginative techniques to achieve the end result.

1. DRAWING AND MASKING

I drew a rough outline with a dark brown water-soluble crayon and, using masking fluid, masked the tree structures using a twig for the trunks and a cocktail stick for the finer lines. These tools were disposable, which saved me the effort of having to remove the masking from brushes. I used a stippling action with a crumpled piece of grease-proof paper dipped in the fluid to mask the foliage. To paint the sky, I poured a Cerulean Blue wash over the area, followed by a Permanent Sap Green wash over the areas of foliage. Both of these washes were pre-mixed in ceramic saucers.

2. BUILDING UP TONE

In order to represent shadows in the foliage, I waited until the washes in stage 1 had completely dried and then poured a dark tone of pre-mixed Permanent Sap Green/Burnt Umber over the lower half of the painting.

3. REMOVING MASKING AND PAINTING THE BUSHES

After removing the masking from the trees and bushes above the bridge by means of a putty eraser, I painted in representations of azaleas and rhododendrons. The colours I used were mixes of Raw Sienna, Cadmium Yellow Pale, Alizarin Crimson and Burnt Sienna, applied with a size 6 round brush.

4. REMOVING MASKING, PAINTING FLOWERS AND WATER

The masking was removed from the lower half of the painting and the flowers painted with mixes of French Ultramarine, Alizarin Crimson, Raw Sienna, Cadmium Yellow Pale, Burnt Sienna and Payne's Gray. Payne's Gray and Alizarin Crimson provided a darker tone as shadows in the foreground bushes. The stream was painted using various tones of a Cerulean Blue/Payne's Gray mix.

5. FINAL STAGE

To complete this painting the background trees were added, using darker tones of green for the left-hand tree and lighter tones for the right-hand tree. A range of soft yellow greens and darker greens were mixed using Cadmium Yellow Pale and Permanent Sap Green. A natural sponge dipped in the mixes was used to stipple in the foliage. A rigger brush loaded with Burnt Umber was used to paint in the tree structures.

The colours used

| Payne's Gray | Cerulean Blue | Alizarin Crimson | Raw Sienna | Burnt Umber | Cadmium Yellow Pale | Permanent Sap Green | Burnt Sienna |

ATMOSPHERE AND MOOD *Introduction*

There's an old saying that 'labourers work with their hands, craftsmen work with their hands and their head, and artists work with their hands, head and *heart*.' This is particularly relevant when creating atmosphere and mood.

Emotions can be stirred by a fast-flowing river, the beauty of falling snow, the effect of light, children playing on a beach or the excitement of colour in a landscape.

Creating atmosphere and mood isn't just attempting to capture a sense of drama such as wind-blown clouds over a dominant mountain structure. It may be a sense of peace and tranquillity, a pastoral scene or the shape of trees in a particular setting. It's what stirs our emotions and provides us with a sense of excitement, contentment, fascination or awe.

It's the artist's role to attempt to capture that special moment in time, using the tools at his disposal.

Diagonal lines provide a sense of movement, as in a wind-blown sky. Vertical lines suggest a sense of awe and power, such as in tall buildings or high mountains. Horizontal lines suggest a pastoral scene. An atmospheric effect can be subtle or bold but the overall effect should be representative of the place you are painting and sympathetic to nature.

In the following pages, I'm going to show you how to paint a wide range of atmospheric effects and encourage you to use your imagination to create paintings that will give you many years of pleasure and satisfaction.

Painting is rather like making a cake – gather all the ingredients together in the best mix and create your masterpiece.

*I painted this evening sky, **From the Road to Mallaig**, by initially applying a Cerulean Blue wash at the top and adding a Raw Sienna/Alizarin Crimson mix as I approached the horizon. When the under-painting was approximately one-third dry, the clouds were painted, using the hake brush loaded with a dark toned Payne's Gray/Alizarin Crimson mix.*

Points to remember

- *Try to create a wide range of atmospheric effects.*
- *Use your imagination.*

The tonal values on the left side of this typical woodland path in **Green Harmony** are darker than those on the right. In the distance the colours are paler and cooler, taking the viewer's eye down the path into the painting. The walkers are the focal point and have been placed to direct the eye.

The colours used

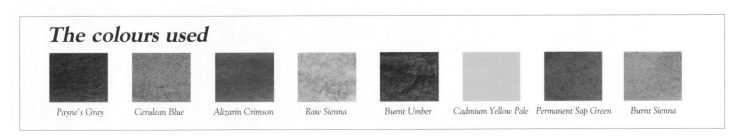

| Payne's Gray | Cerulean Blue | Alizarin Crimson | Raw Sienna | Burnt Umber | Cadmium Yellow Pale | Permanent Sap Green | Burnt Sienna |

ATMOSPHERE AND MOOD *The effect of light*

It can be an informative and enjoyable experience to paint the same scene at different times of the day. The changing light has significant effects on the landscape, creating contrasts in atmosphere and mood. Compare these paintings of the same scene in early morning, at midday and in early evening.

Early Morning *Blue-green mixes and simple washes were used here to clearly define the time of day.*

The shadows are ill-defined, and the subtle distinctions between the elements lack sharpness. The colours tend to a bluish green and there's a suggestion of mist that will quickly disappear as the sun rises.

I painted a wet into wet sky, using Cerulean Blue, and added a weak Permanent Sap Green to the blue to paint the distant trees. Various tones of these two colours were used to paint the foreground trees and bushes, the land and also the water.

Midday *The clarity of this landscape suggests that it's noon. Any early morning mist has been burnt off by the warmth of the sun. A division between the lights and darks can easily be seen. There's a greater contrast in colours and tones because the light is stronger.*

I used combinations of French Ultramarine, Cadmium Yellow Pale, Raw Sienna and a Payne's Gray for the trees and painted warmer colours in the land areas. The sunlight is reflected in the water.

Late Evening *The sun is beginning to set. The elements are silhouetted against the warmth of the sky and there's less detail to be seen. The water reflects the colours of the sky. Night is rapidly approaching. In a short time the landscape will fade into darkness. Everything is at rest; the birds have gone to roost and the fishermen are enjoying peace and quiet, away from the stresses of life.*

The colours I used to paint this scene were Cadmium Yellow Pale, Raw Sienna, Alizarin Crimson and Burnt Umber.

EXERCISES

• Select a local scene, within your present competence level, and paint it at different times of the day. Make notes of the principal differences in terms of light, cloud structures, colour contrasts, tonal values and sharpness.

• Take lots of photographs of interesting cloud formations to build up a resource from which you can draw as and.when required.

• Study the effect rain clouds have on the colours in the landscape.

• Choose a landscape painting in this book and paint it as if it were a depiction of another season.

• Practise painting sheep, figures and boats.

Autumn Light *depicts the changing colours of autumn. Note the variety of colours in the foliage and the effect of light in the atmospheric sky radiating over the mountain range.*

Because this is a back-lit subject, shadows are cast in the water.

Points to remember

• An atmospheric effect can be subtle or bold, but the overall impression should be representative of the region and sympathetic to nature.
• When painting early morning, shadows are ill-defined and the subtle distinctions between the elements lack sharpness.
• In the evening shapes become silhouettes against a soft, warm sky.
• The sky sets the scene in a painting, creating atmosphere and mood.

• Fog and mist cast a veil over distant objects; colours are softened and the elements appear diffused. Distant fog or mist can be emphasized by adding in the foreground a little more detail and colour than can actually be seen.
• When painting snow always establish the value relationships between the sky and its reflections in the snow.
• To paint rain, apply a wet initial wash, paint in the cloud colours, lift the board and tilt it to encourage the paint to run in the direction required. When you are satisfied with the result, lay the board flat and allow the paint to dry naturally.

ATMOSPHERE AND MOOD *Skies and rain clouds*

The sky establishes the atmosphere and mood in a painting. The effects of light in the landscape are vital to bring your watercolours to life. Don't forget that practice makes perfect – you're not expected to get it right first time.

When I want to emphasize the effects of light in the landscape and to help me create atmosphere and mood, I will take photographs that go against the usual conventions of photography. Rather than having the sun behind me as convention dictates, I will shoot looking directly into the sun. The photographs will print much darker but the contrasting lights and darks will be very distinctive. I will use different camera settings, and then assess the results.

Try this approach for yourself. When you come to apply paint to your subject, it will be up to you to create the atmosphere and mood you want.

The sky in **Scottish Loch** *was painted with the same technique as that used in* **Snow Capped**. *The colours used were Raw Sienna, French Ultramarine and Alizarin Crimson.*

Snow Capped is a dramatic sky painted with a hake brush. A circle of Cadmium Yellow Pale was painted to represent light radiating from the sun. Mixes of Cerulean Blue/Payne's Gray and Alizarin Crimson were used to paint various tones of colour in the sky. While the paint was still very wet the paper was tilted to allow the colours to flow and blend together.

The dramatic sky in **Not Quite There** *was painted in less than four minutes. A greater variety of colours and tones was used for this sky study than for the other two shown on this page: Raw Sienna for the under-painting, followed by Cerulean/French Ultramarine mixes and Payne's Gray/Alizarin Crimson to create the darker tones. A few white clouds were created by removing paint with an absorbent tissue.*

A sky full of rain is possibly the easiest type to paint with watercolours. Attach your watercolour paper to a board and lay it flat, apply a very wet wash of a pale tone of Cerulean Blue or Raw Sienna and, while the paper is still very wet, brush in dark tones of Payne's Gray mixed with Raw Sienna, Burnt Umber or Alizarin Crimson at the top of your paper. Immediately, lift up the board and paper and, holding them almost vertical, tilt them in the direction required to encourage the paint to flow. Watch the result as you do this, and once the paint has run sufficiently to create the effect you're looking for, lay the paper perfectly flat and let the paint dry naturally. Use a tissue to soak up any unwanted pools of colour at the bottom of the sky. It's as easy as that.

This technique was used for both of the paintings shown below.

Homeward Bound was started in the English Lake District while my wife held an umbrella over me. Such weather conditions encourage speedy work.

For the sky, I quickly brushed in a weak Cerulean Blue and added a little Raw Sienna in selected areas, followed by a Payne's Gray/Raw Sienna mix. The shepherd and sheep were painted in my studio later.

The House on the Moor offers you an opportunity to practise the technique I use for depicting a rainy landscape. Although the technique is very easy, timing is important. Only experience through practice will teach you how to get this right.

To paint the sky, wet the area initially with a weak Raw Sienna or Cerulean Blue, and use a mix of Payne's Gray/Raw Sienna for the clouds.

Wet and Windy is full of atmosphere and mood. The rain is streaking down. The distant mountains are barely discernible through the torrential rain and this gives them a ghostly appearance. It's not the day to be out and about. The smoke from the chimney indicates that those living in the croft are of the same opinion. I think you will enjoy painting this scene.

THE SKY

I fastened the paper to the board and laid it flat before painting the rain clouds. I used a hake brush to apply a very wet Cerulean Blue wash to the whole of the sky area. While the under-painting was still wet, a strong mix of Payne's Gray with a little Burnt Umber added was brushed into the top of the sky. The board was immediately lifted and angled vertically to allow the paint to run down the paper. Once the desired effect was achieved the board was laid perfectly flat and the paint left to dry naturally.

MOUNTAINS AND BUILDINGS

I fastened the paper to the board and laid it flat before painting the rain clouds. I used a hake brush to apply a very wet Cerulean Blue wash to the whole of the sky area. While the under-painting was still wet, a strong mix of Payne's Gray with a little Burnt Umber added was brushed into the top of the sky. The board was immediately lifted and angled vertically to allow the paint to run down the paper. Once the desired effect was achieved the board was laid perfectly flat and the paint left to dry naturally.

Atmosphere

In this painting the atmosphere is created almost entirely by the rain clouds and their effect on the landscape.

ROCKS

After removing the masking the rocks were painted using Raw Sienna as an under-painting and Payne's Gray/Burnt Umber for the shadows. Highlights were made by removing paint from the tops of the rocks with a tissue rolled to a point. Dark shadows were painted under the rocks to make them look more realistic.

ATMOSPHERE AND MOOD *Mist, fog and snow*

Fog and mist cast a veil over objects in the distance and colours appear soft and diffused. It's important to keep distant values light in tone and add a little more colour and definition in the foreground. The foreground must be more sharply focussed than it appears in reality to give emphasis to the mist or fog in the background

*The sky for **Lakeside** was painted wet into wet, by applying a weak Cerulean Blue wash and brushing in some Alizarin Crimson. I continued working downwards and painted the water using the same colours. While the paint was still wet, I painted the distant mountains and the trees in the middle distance, wet into wet, to achieve a soft diffused look. The fir trees were painted with a stiffer Permanent Sap Green, then I used a tissue to remove some colour and soften the tree grouping. Reflections using very pale colours were added to the water while the paint was still wet. When the paint was dry the land and rocks in the foreground were painted in more detail to lead the viewer's eye into the painting.*

Mist on the River *depicts an early morning scene, with the sun struggling to shine through the mist. The sketch has been painted wet into wet to achieve the soft, filtered light effect that is so necessary when painting mist or fog. My aim was to create a hazy atmospheric effect. The colours used were Cadmium Yellow Pale, Raw Sienna, Payne's Gray, Alizarin Crimson, Cerulean Blue and Burnt Sienna.*

When painting snow it's important to establish the value relationships between the snow and the sky. Snow isn't always white, just as the sky is not always a pretty blue. Leave the paper untouched for the whitest snow. The washes used for the sky can be transferred to the snow area to create the shadows reflected from passing clouds.

Snow scenes don't have to look cold. You can use soft washes of Cerulean Blue for a cold scene, a purple hue made from Payne's Gray or French Ultramarine and Alizarin Crimson for a slightly warmer effect, and for warmer sunlit snow you can apply a Raw Sienna glaze over a blue or purple underpainting. Show some stubble, tufts of grass or even the odd rock protruding through the snow to add interest.

In the following two examples, you'll notice how important are the skies to the success of the paintings.

Early Snow depicts the first coating of snow on the landscape. The subject is back-lit; I have painted a little Raw Sienna into the sky to reflect this, and have also transferred some of this colour into the snow lying on the fields. Note how I have achieved recession by painting the trees and bushes in the far distance in cooler pale tones.

To paint the stubble and vegetation showing through the light covering of snow, I used the edge of a hake brush, touching the paper lightly with an upward flicking motion.

In *On Thurstaston Hill*, a favourite beauty spot in the Wirral, where I live, I have used the sky colours of Payne's Gray and Alizarin Crimson to paint the path and the pool of water on the right. This was important to achieve colour harmony in the scene. The white of the paper has been left uncovered to represent snow at ground level. I used a little white acrylic paint to stipple the effects of snow on the trees and foreground gorse bushes.

ATMOSPHERE AND MOOD *Close up*

There's nothing quite like a walk in the woods on a crisp winter's day. Nature in all its glory is a joy to behold. **Woodland Walk** is one such scene, providing the opportunity to incorporate a soft atmospheric sky, a wide variation in the colours of winter and the effects of a light dusting of snow on the landscape. This is the type of scene I love to paint. I used acrylic watercolours to paint it.

SKY AND IVY

I painted the sky by initially applying a pale Raw Sienna wash over the sky area with a hake brush. Using downward strokes, I then brushed in Cerulean Blue, starting on the left and gradually changing to a soft purple as I worked my way across to the right of the painting. I left some of the Raw Sienna uncovered to represent the sun breaking through a diffused background. When the paint was approximately one-third dry, I painted the distant trees, using a stiffer mix of Payne's Gray/Permanent Sap Green to achieve a blurred effect to lead the viewer's eye into the distance.

The ivy on the trees was painted with a hog-hair brush using a stippling technique; dark tones of Burnt Umber/Permanent Sap Green were applied, followed by a paler, brighter green and finally white acrylic paint stippled on to give the effect of snow.

TREES AND SHADOWS

Using a rigger brush, the trunks and branches were initially painted with pale Raw Sienna. When the paint was approximately one-third dry, some dark tones of Burnt Umber were added to make the branches look realistic. The soft purple mix for the sky was also used to paint the shadows on the path, using the side of the round brush.

Snow

Using white acrylic paint is only one way of representing snow. There are other techniques – *see page 31.*

FOREGROUND TEXTURE

I lightly stippled a variety of colours using the edge of a hake brush, and left some white of the paper uncovered. I applied soft greens and Raw Sienna in the main and added a small amount of Payne's Gray for the darker tones. Finally, a little white has been stippled with a hog-hair brush to soften areas where the snow has drifted into the stubble.

1.

2.

In **Snow on the River** I'm going to show you a variety of watercolour techniques and how they can be combined to produce a successful painting.

1. MASKING AND POURING

After preparing the initial tonal study to establish the lights and darks and completing a simple drawing, I masked the tree shapes, the highlights I wanted to retain in the water and areas representing snow on the banks as well as areas of foliage.

Two washes were mixed in ceramic saucers, one using Cadmium Yellow Pale and one a mixture of Payne's Gray and Alizarin Crimson. The Cadmium Yellow mix was poured down the right-hand side of the painting and the Payne's Gray/Alizarin Crimson wash poured down the left-hand side. The board with the watercolour paper attached was inclined at a slight angle to allow the washes to flow down, blend together and run off the bottom of the paper.

2. PAINTING TREES

When the paint used in the first stage was dry, I painted the distant trees in light tones of Payne's Gray/Alizarin Crimson. Mixes of Raw Sienna and Burnt Sienna were applied to represent the bushes in the middle distance. I used the side of a size 14 round brush to paint the bushes. The fir trees were painted using a flat brush loaded with mixes of Permanent Sap Green and Payne's Gray.

3. REMOVING MASKING

Once the painting was completely dry, I removed the masking fluid by means of gentle rubbing with a putty eraser.

4. ADDING DETAILS

The tree shapes were painted with a rigger brush by applying a Raw Sienna wash over the trunks, followed by deposits of Burnt Umber to make them look natural. Using the sky colours, I painted shadows over the snow. The rocks were painted with a flat brush: Raw Sienna for their under-painting and Payne's Gray/Alizarin Crimson for the shadows under the rocks and in the water. To complete this stage, washes of Cadmium Yellow Pale, Raw Sienna and a weak Alizarin Crimson/Raw Sienna mix were painted over the white of the paper which had been restored after the removal of the masking from the trees and bushes.

The colours used

| Payne's Gray | Alizarin Crimson | Raw Sienna | Burnt Umber | Cadmium Yellow Pale | Permanent Sap Green | Burnt Sienna |

3.

4.

5. BALANCING TONE AND COLOUR

To complete this painting, I added a few more rocks in the river, painted darker tones of Payne's Gray/Alizarin Crimson underneath the trees and bushes and painted the foliage on the two young trees on the right-hand side. I also added several fir trees in the distance and a large boulder in the right foreground. Small amounts of white acrylic paint were applied to the trees to represent snow.

We've already seen how useful it can be to include a feature in your painting other than what nature provides in the shape of the elements and the landscape. Many of the more common details are easy enough to paint. I'll show you how below.

SHEEP

When you come to paint sheep, think horseshoes. If the sheep is looking to the right, add a second horseshoe to extend the body to the right and then a triangle for the head. Naturally it is the same process only reversed if the animal is looking to the left – extending the body to the left and adding a triangle for its head. I use Payne's Gray/Burnt Umber to block in and then over-paint with either white acrylic paint or gouache. It's essential to add shadows beneath your sheep to make them look realistic.

FIGURES

So you think you can't paint figures? If you follow the steps shown, you'll find it easy. Before adding figures to your painting, it's a good idea to draw them first on clear film or tracing paper using a felt tip pen and then place this over your painting to determine the best position for them.

BOATS

Follow the simple stages shown and soon you will be competent to add boats to your paintings.

BUILDINGS

Here I have simplified the painting of a building. The dotted lines are included to help you simplify your drawing and show you how vanishing points go off into the distance. Linear perspective is the key to making your buildings look realistic.

To become a successful artist it's essential to understand tonal values, which I believe to be the most important contributing factor to painting a successful landscape.

All paintings need contrasts of tone and the balance between lights and darks arranged in relationships that enhance the quality of the painting. Many beginners tend to splash paint on without any preliminary thought about the design of their painting, and as a result what they produce looks flat and uninteresting.

It has always been my practice to clarify my thinking by producing small tonal sketches, using a dark brown water-soluble crayon. These sketches are only 3 x 4.5 inches in size and display little detail. Their purpose is to help me choose the best view of the landscape I am about to paint and to establish the best combination of light and darks. These tonal studies are simple scribbles but are vital to the success of my painting. If you produce tonal sketches to clarify your thinking before you apply paint, I guarantee that your paintings will improve significantly.

Utilizing Tonal Values

The following are two distinct ways in which tonal values can be successfully utilized in a painting, to ensure that your work never looks flat:

Counterchange is an effective way to highlight the principal subject matter in a painting, such as the focal point. By emphasizing lights against darks and darks against lights, interesting features can be made more distinctive. Examples could be: surrounding the light in a sky with darker contrasting tones of colour to make the light source appear brighter; painting a light toned figure against the dark background of a building; or painting dark trees behind the light toned roof of a building.

Gradation occurs when a colour gradually changes, either from a light tone to a darker tone or the reverse. Examples could be the transition in colour from foreground grass to that in the distance or the transition in colour from wet to dry sand on a beach.

Autumn Fields was painted on a warm, early autumn day. The focal point was the lone tree on the left. Darker tones were painted into this to make it more distinctive. Note the variation in tonal values in the grass areas, necessary to create realism in the scene. The distant trees were painted in lighter tones to achieve recession. The variety of colours and tones in the right-hand tree grouping gives structure and depth to the painting. The dark posts and bush on the left-hand bank serve to balance the larger tree grouping on the right.

How to transfer an outline drawing of a completed painting onto watercolour paper

The next technique is not a substitute for learning to draw and should only be used until you are competent at drawing.

1. Take a black and white photocopy of the painting to the size required.

2. Using a soft pencil (6B), scribble across the back of the photocopy.

3. Position the photocopy over your watercolour paper, trace around the outline and key features using a biro or 2H pencil.

4. Remove the photocopy. The image will have transferred to your paper ready for you to apply paint.

ATMOSPHERE, MOOD AND LIGHT *Close up*

Peace and Tranquillity depicts Scotland's salmon country. I was inspired by the atmospheric sky and the variety of tree species. The mountains provided the backcloth to the painting.

The only problem I encountered when painting this scene was presented by the many rocks in the river, which were time-consuming to paint.

I hope you enjoy painting this scene.

FIR TREES

Fir trees are quite easy to paint; simply use a flat brush and stipple, working upwards from ground level. As you stipple, rock the brush from side to side to define the shape, using more of the corner of the brush as you progress up each tree. Varying tones of Permanent Sap Green and Payne's Gray were used.

A number of bushes were painted in front of the fir trees to add variety of height, tone and colour. Some highlights were added to the foliage on the fir trees where the light reflected, using a mix of Cadmium Yellow and Permanent Sap Green with a little acrylic white added.

SKY AND MOUNTAINS

The sky is an important feature in this painting. The light from the sky softened the mountain structure and created sparkle on the surface of the water.

Skies such as this are easily painted. Apply the usual Raw Sienna wash, brush in the cloud shapes with, in this case, varying tones of blue and, to create the light effects, dab out some of the colour with a tissue to produce the feathery white clouds.

The mountains were painted with a hake brush, using sweeping directional strokes from peak to ground level. Shape your mountains by means of a tissue formed into a tight wedge, creating light areas by applying downward strokes at an approximate angle of 45° following the structure of the mountain. The colours used were Raw Sienna, Payne's Gray and Permanent Sap Green.

TREES, ROCKS AND RUNNING WATER

On the left bank were various young trees, their leaves changing colour as autumn approached. I stippled with a round hog-hair brush to create realistic looking foliage, using mixes made from Raw Sienna, Burnt Sienna, Permanent Sap Green and Payne's Gray.

When painting water it's a useful technique to partially close your eyes to allow observation of the various tones more clearly. A hake brush was used to paint the water, using Cerulean Blue/Payne's Gray mixes, taking care to leave lots of white paper uncovered to represent the light shimmering on the water.

A flat brush is ideal for shaping rocks. Paint a few of them at a time, applying a wash of Raw Sienna, followed by darker tones of Burnt Umber to give them shape. Don't forget to paint shadows under the rocks or they will look as if they are floating on the surface. This attention to detail distinguishes the more experienced painter from the beginner.

SPRING

It's spring, the new shoots are appearing, there's a fresh glow in the distance and the bluebells are in bloom. The birds are singing and everything in nature seems clean and new. Spring heralds the beginning of the artist's year.

When painting woodland scenes it's important to paint a simple sky that doesn't detract from the foreground detail. You must also design your painting so that the viewer's eye is taken beyond the foreground and into the distance. In this example I have used the path to lead the eye into the painting and out around the bend in the distance.

It's important to be able to paint a wide variety of greens. With four colours it's possible to mix over one hundred shades of green. For example, mix Payne's Gray and Raw Sienna together with varying quantities of water and you will create a range of very dark greens, olive greens and yellow greens. By mixing Cadmium Yellow Pale with Payne's Gray you will get a wide range of grass- and yellow-greens in dark and medium tones. Using Payne's Gray (the darkest blue) produces colours that are basically dark in tone, which makes them ideal for capturing shadows and depth.

In this painting a range of bright, sparkling greens was produced by experimenting with mixes of Cerulean Blue or French Ultramarine with Cadmium Yellow Pale. Cerulean Blue mixed with Raw Sienna will give yellow greens.

There are two techniques for painting bluebells. You can apply masking fluid, over-paint with greens, remove the masking and then paint over the white of the paper with French Ultramarine. Alternatively, you can paint the banks and when these are dry, over-paint with some white acrylic paint or gouache mixed with French Ultramarine. I chose the latter technique for this detail.

SUMMER

It's summertime and the tree structures can barely be seen due to the abundance of foliage. At ground level the grasses are in full growth and surrounding bushes are waiting for the young birds to leave their nests. The range of greens and siennas used to depict this woodland scene creates splashes of colour. The trees in full leaf cast shadows across the path, leading the eye into the distance.

Trees appear dark on the inside with light foliage sparkling on the outside. The water colourist paints light to dark, which conflicts with the previous statement and what is observed in nature.

My method when painting trees is to follow convention but after I have added darker tones to create depth, I will finish with touches of bright colour to soften the effect and create highlights.

Don't use black for shadows. Mix 20 per cent of any colour on your palette with 80 per cent Payne's Gray and you will produce an extensive range of blue, brown, red or green shadow colours that can be used where appropriate. My personal favourite for tree shadows is a mix of Payne's Gray with a small amount of Alizarin Crimson added.

To paint the grasses, I used a soft yellow green wash and stippled with darker tones of green using a hake and a hog-hair brush. I used a small natural sponge dipped in paint to stipple on the foliage. For the final highlights, I stippled with a round hog-hair brush once the under-painting had dried.

In this vignette, I used combinations of Cadmium Yellow Pale, Cerulean Blue, Raw Sienna, Burnt Umber and Payne's Gray.

ATMOSPHERE, MOOD AND LIGHT *The seasons*

AUTUMN

It is now autumn, my favourite time of year. The leaves have changed colour, and are now displaying a wonderful array of soft yellows to deep red-browns. Nature's colours are at their best at this time of year, and offer the landscape painter an abundance of majestic scenes to paint as well as opportunities to experiment with colour mixing.

As the trees change from their summer to autumn colours the woodland displays a great variety of soft greens, yellows, siennas, ochres and rich red-browns. Only touches of green are evident.

The less experienced painter will find the representation of foliage most difficult, whether they want to paint loosely or in great detail. In this painting the foliage was painted with a sponge, using a stippling technique.

The benefits of painting the same scene

Painting the same scene at different times of the year can be a fascinating and illuminating experience. It's both exciting and beneficial to your development as a landscape painter because it teaches you so much about colour mixing and gives you practice in a range of different techniques.

To paint this vignette, I mixed various colours from the selection of Cadmium Yellow Pale, Raw Sienna, Alizarin Crimson, Burnt Sienna, Burnt Umber and Payne's Gray.

WINTER

Winter has arrived. The leaves have fallen, except for a few determined to keep their lofty positions. The distant woodland appears diffused, yet the glory of what had been can still be seen in the occasional splash of colour. The ground is lightly covered in snow, with the young saplings and stubble projecting upwards.

Such a scene demands a simple background sky. In this example, a few downward strokes of a hake brush loaded with Cerulean Blue over a Raw Sienna under-painting sufficed. The painting will look too fussy if a complex sky is painted. Remember the 'Golden Rule': a detailed foreground demands a simple sky – a simple foreground requires an atmospheric sky.

The background trees were painted wet into wet, to create a diffused effect. This was achieved by using the corner of a hake brush, when the sky was approximately one-third dry. I scratched in the tree structures using a palette knife; a cocktail stick would also have done the job.

Timing is vital here. If the tree structures are to look almost white, the under-painting must not be too wet otherwise the paint will run back and you'll get dark tones. Experience will tell you when the time is right to begin scratching out.

This vignette shows the technique I used for painting the tree trunks. I defined the structure of the trees first by drawing them with a flat brush loaded with raw sienna. When the paint was approximately one-third dry, I removed some colour from the length of the trunk with a tissue shaped to a point. Finally, I used a rigger brush to paint some detail on the trunk using darker tones of Payne's Gray/Burnt Umber.

43

When writing these books, it was never my intention to attempt to impose a style of painting on anyone, but rather to show different techniques which would allow you to stamp your own style on your paintings with both confidence and pleasure. I like to think of an artist's style as being akin to handwriting in paint. You may wish to paint in a loose, free style or perhaps represent the landscape in detail. Over time you will develop your own style of painting – it can't be imposed on you.

Woodland Beck incorporates all the techniques described in this book. I used acrylic watercolours, but I could have used traditional watercolour paints just as easily.

FOLIAGE

After the tree structures were drawn in, the foliage was painted by initially stippling dark tones of a Payne's Gray/Permanent Sap Green mix. When this dark under-painting was dry, lighter greens were stippled over it. I used a round hog-hair brush (oil painter's brush) for this technique. The beauty of acrylics is that you can easily work light to dark or dark to light.

WATER

Initially I painted the fast-flowing water between the rocks. This was done by dipping the hairs of a round brush in Payne's Gray and then fanning them between thumb and finger to create irregular sections. The fine hairs were then quickly brushed between the rocks, which had the effect of leaving white paper uncovered to represent the running water.

I used a round, pointed brush with mixes of Payne's Gray and Cerulean Blue to add a variety of tones to complete the beck. The strokes were horizontal in direction. A little Raw Sienna was brushed in to represent reflections from the background light.

TEXTURE

There's considerable detailed texture in this painting to reflect the plant life you find when walking through woodland – tufts of grass, young bushes and saplings and, in this case, a carpet of bluebells.

Over the years, I have experimented with various brushes to achieve a natural look for depictions of a woodland floor. I find that stippling with an old oil painter's brush gives my preferred result, and I've used this method here.

Every artist dedicated to their work will be continually experimenting with new techniques to create paintings that stir their emotions. You might be fired to capture a sense of realism, the beauty of nature's creation or simply to complete a painting with which you are happy.

Experimentation is important if you want to be able to call on a wide range of techniques in your paintings. I have been able to produce several interesting landscapes by using different techniques, such as controlling the flow of paint with masking fluid or masking tape, pouring paint from saucers, scumbling, glazing, knifing out or spattering.

Autumn Flow is one such painting. I'm delighted to have the opportunity to show you some of the techniques I used to paint it.

1. MASKING AND POURING

An initial tonal study was completed and the outline of the painting drawn. Masking was applied by brush to the mountains and the water and to the foliage with a crumpled piece of grease-proof paper. A cocktail stick dipped in masking fluid was used to draw the tree structures.

The sky was painted with a hake brush loaded with mixes of Cerulean Blue and Alizarin Crimson and then allowed to dry.

The mountain was painted using a weak mixture of Payne's Gray and Alizarin Crimson and allowed to dry.

Washes of Raw Sienna, Burnt Sienna and Payne's Gray were pre-mixed in ceramic saucers and poured over the tree areas after the tops of the rocks had been masked out with a piece of masking tape to prevent the washes from running below this line. The board was tilted to allow the washes to run slowly and merge together. The paper was then laid flat to dry, with a hair dryer eventually used to ensure the paint was completely dry.

2. ESTABLISHING TONAL VALUES

Further pourings of the paint added depth to the trees. When this was dry the rough shapes of the fir trees were painted with a flat brush loaded with a Permanent Sap Green/Payne's Gray mix. The distant fir trees on the left were painted using a weaker mix.

3. REMOVING THE MASKING

The distant mountains were given more definition by applying a Payne's Gray/Alizarin Crimson wash. When this was dry a putty eraser was used to remove the masking from the mountains and the areas of foliage.

Painting the rocks is a very easy process, and comes next. Washes of Raw Sienna followed by Burnt Sienna and Payne's Gray are applied to selected areas. A palette knife is then used to shape the rocks. The paint isn't applied with the knife but simply moved around to create the shape of the rocks. At the end of each stroke of the knife, the build up of paint leaves a dark edge, representing shadows. The paper isn't damaged in any way by this.

Finally the masking was removed from the waterfall and the waterfall painted in a Payne's Gray/Cerulean Blue mix using light strokes with a hake brush following the direction of flow. The rocks projecting through the water were painted using a flat brush loaded with the colours used previously.

4. ADDING DETAIL

It's time to bring the painting together and add the finishing touches. Raw Sienna, Cadmium Yellow Pale and Burnt Sienna glazes were applied to the foliage and tree structures. These same glazes were also used to colour the rocks and create depth of tone.

Highlights to the foliage were then applied. Paper masks had to be first cut to shape to protect other areas, such as the sky; I used a piece of mounting card cut to various profiles to fit around the trees. To apply the paint, I took an old toothbrush, dipped it in Cadmium Yellow Pale, ran my thumb over the bristles and then spattered the colour onto the foliage.

Taking time to get it right

I rarely complete a painting in one sitting. I prefer to work on it over several days, looking at it critically and making any changes I feel are necessary. I might remove paint to lighten areas or apply glazes (a little paint mixed with lots of water) to improve the variation of colour and tone.

Using the above process, I have been able to produce several interesting landscapes and enjoy this different approach to painting. I recommend you try these methods – above all, have fun and enjoy your painting.

The colours used

| Payne's Gray | Alizarin Crimson | Raw Sienna | Cerulean Blue | Cadmium Yellow Pale | Permanent Sap Green | Burnt Sienna |

PORTRAIT OF THE ARTIST

Keith Fenwick is one of the UK's leading teachers of painting techniques. He enjoys a tremendous following among leisure painters, who flock to his demonstrations and workshops at major fine art and craft shows.

Keith is a Chartered Engineer, a Fellow of the Royal Society of Arts, an Advisory Panel member of the Society for All Artists and holds several professional qualifications including an honours degree. He served an engineering apprenticeship, becoming chief draughtsman, before progressing to senior management in both industry and further education. He took early retirement from his position as Associate Principal/Director of Sites and Publicity at one of the UK's largest colleges of further education in order to devote more time to his great love, landscape painting.

Keith's paintings are in collections in the United Kingdom and other European countries, as well as in the United States, Canada, New Zealand, Australia, Japan and the Middle East.

Keith runs painting holidays in the UK and Europe, seminars and workshops nationwide and demonstrates to up to 50 art societies each year. Keith can be seen demonstrating painting techniques at most major fine art and craft shows in the UK. He has had a long and fruitful association with Winsor & Newton, for whom he is a principal demonstrator.

Keith's expertise in landscape painting, his writings, teaching, video-making and broadcasting ensure an understanding of student needs. His book *Seasonal Landscapes* has proved very popular, as have his 20 best-selling art teaching videos, which have benefited students worldwide. He is a regular contributor to art and craft magazines.

Keith finds great satisfaction in encouraging those who have always wanted to paint but lack the confidence to have a go, as well as helping more experienced painters to develop their skills further. He hopes this series will be a constant companion to those wishing to improve their skills and experiment with new ways to paint the landscape.